Forever GRATEFUL.

A 90-DAY GRATITUDE & REFLECTION JOURNAL

Forever Grateful. A 90-Day Gratitude & Reflection Journal
Copyright © 2022 Golden Seed Press, LLC. All rights reserved. This book or any portion thereof may not be reproduced or used in any manner except for brief excerpts for reviews and commentaries without the express written permission of the publisher.

Connect: info@goldenseedpress.com
IG: @thegoldenseedpress
Written and designed by: Shaliss Monet Wilkes
Connect: shalissmonet.com
Cover image original: aradaphotography

ISBN - 979-8-9870572-2-3

This journal belongs to

_____

I am *Forever* GRATEFUL.

There is beauty within every new day. And for every stressor and strain, there is something to be thankful for, something to celebrate, be it big or seemingly small.

Practicing gratitude is like moving the clouds aside and allowing the sun to shine through just a little bit more. If you are not naturally bent toward expressing thankfulness, or if you are in a dark season of life and need help seeing the good around you, this 90-day practice in gratitude and reflection may help you lean more toward the light.

Complete one page daily and begin to live *Forever Grateful.*

Date   /   /   Su Mo Tu We Th Fr Sa

Today, I am grateful for...

What good, beautiful, or pleasantly surprising thing happened today?

How can you/did you bring joy to someone else today?

Write out a prayer of gratitude or set positive intentions.

Date   /   /   Su Mo Tu We Th Fr Sa

Today, I am grateful for...
_____
_____
_____
_____

What good, beautiful, or pleasantly surprising thing happened today?
_____
_____
_____
_____

How can you/did you bring joy to someone else today?
_____
_____
_____
_____

Write out a prayer of gratitude or set positive intentions.
_____
_____
_____
_____

Date   /   /   Su Mo Tu We Th Fr Sa

Today, I am grateful for...
_____
_____
_____
_____
_____

What good, beautiful, or pleasantly surprising thing happened today?
_____
_____
_____
_____
_____

How can you/did you bring joy to someone else today?
_____
_____
_____
_____
_____

Write out a prayer of gratitude or set positive intentions.
_____
_____
_____
_____

Date   /   /   Su Mo Tu We Th Fr Sa

Today, I am grateful for...
_____
_____
_____
_____

What good, beautiful, or pleasantly surprising thing happened today?
_____
_____
_____
_____

How can you/did you bring joy to someone else today?
_____
_____
_____
_____

Write out a prayer of gratitude or set positive intentions.
_____
_____
_____
_____

Date   /   /   Su Mo Tu We Th Fr Sa

Today, I am grateful for...
_____
_____
_____
_____
_____

What good, beautiful, or pleasantly surprising thing happened today?
_____
_____
_____
_____
_____

How can you/did you bring joy to someone else today?
_____
_____
_____
_____
_____

Write out a prayer of gratitude or set positive intentions.
_____
_____
_____
_____

Date   /   /   Su Mo Tu We Th Fr Sa

Today, I am grateful for...
___
___
___
___
___

What good, beautiful, or pleasantly surprising thing happened today?
___
___
___
___
___

How can you/did you bring joy to someone else today?
___
___
___
___
___

Write out a prayer of gratitude or set positive intentions.
___
___
___
___

Date   /   /   Su Mo Tu We Th Fr Sa

Today, I am grateful for...

What good, beautiful, or pleasantly surprising thing happened today?

How can you/did you bring joy to someone else today?

Write out a prayer of gratitude or set positive intentions.

Date   /   /   Su Mo Tu We Th Fr Sa

Today, I am grateful for...
_____
_____
_____
_____
_____

What good, beautiful, or pleasantly surprising thing happened today?
_____
_____
_____
_____
_____

How can you/did you bring joy to someone else today?
_____
_____
_____
_____
_____

Write out a prayer of gratitude or set positive intentions.
_____
_____
_____
_____
_____

Date   /   /   Su Mo Tu We Th Fr Sa

Today, I am grateful for...

What good, beautiful, or pleasantly surprising thing happened today?

How can you/did you bring joy to someone else today?

Write out a prayer of gratitude or set positive intentions.

Date   /   /   Su Mo Tu We Th Fr Sa

Today, I am grateful for...
_____
_____
_____
_____
_____

What good, beautiful, or pleasantly surprising thing happened today?
_____
_____
_____
_____
_____

How can you/did you bring joy to someone else today?
_____
_____
_____
_____
_____

Write out a prayer of gratitude or set positive intentions.
_____
_____
_____
_____

Date   /   /   Su Mo Tu We Th Fr Sa

Today, I am grateful for...
_____
_____
_____
_____
_____

What good, beautiful, or pleasantly surprising thing happened today?
_____
_____
_____
_____
_____

How can you/did you bring joy to someone else today?
_____
_____
_____
_____
_____

Write out a prayer of gratitude or set positive intentions.
_____
_____
_____
_____

Date   /   /   Su Mo Tu We Th Fr Sa

Today, I am grateful for...
_____
_____
_____
_____
_____

What good, beautiful, or pleasantly surprising thing happened today?
_____
_____
_____
_____
_____

How can you/did you bring joy to someone else today?
_____
_____
_____
_____
_____

Write out a prayer of gratitude or set positive intentions.
_____
_____
_____
_____

Date   /   /   Su Mo Tu We Th Fr Sa

Today, I am grateful for...
_____
_____
_____
_____
_____

What good, beautiful, or pleasantly surprising thing happened today?
_____
_____
_____
_____
_____

How can you/did you bring joy to someone else today?
_____
_____
_____
_____
_____

Write out a prayer of gratitude or set positive intentions.
_____
_____
_____
_____

Date   /   /   Su Mo Tu We Th Fr Sa

Today, I am grateful for...

What good, beautiful, or pleasantly surprising thing happened today?

How can you/did you bring joy to someone else today?

Write out a prayer of gratitude or set positive intentions.

Date   /   /   Su Mo Tu We Th Fr Sa

Today, I am grateful for...

What good, beautiful, or pleasantly surprising thing happened today?

How can you/did you bring joy to someone else today?

Write out a prayer of gratitude or set positive intentions.

Date   /   /   Su Mo Tu We Th Fr Sa

Today, I am grateful for...

What good, beautiful, or pleasantly surprising thing happened today?

How can you/did you bring joy to someone else today?

Write out a prayer of gratitude or set positive intentions.

Date   /   /   Su Mo Tu We Th Fr Sa

Today, I am grateful for...

What good, beautiful, or pleasantly surprising thing happened today?

How can you/did you bring joy to someone else today?

Write out a prayer of gratitude or set positive intentions.

Date   /   /   Su Mo Tu We Th Fr Sa

Today, I am grateful for...
_____
_____
_____
_____
_____

What good, beautiful, or pleasantly surprising thing happened today?
_____
_____
_____
_____
_____

How can you/did you bring joy to someone else today?
_____
_____
_____
_____
_____

Write out a prayer of gratitude or set positive intentions.
_____
_____
_____
_____
_____

Date   /   /   Su Mo Tu We Th Fr Sa

Today, I am grateful for...
_____
_____
_____
_____
_____

What good, beautiful, or pleasantly surprising thing happened today?
_____
_____
_____
_____
_____

How can you/did you bring joy to someone else today?
_____
_____
_____
_____
_____

Write out a prayer of gratitude or set positive intentions.
_____
_____
_____
_____
_____

Date   /   /   Su Mo Tu We Th Fr Sa

Today, I am grateful for...
_____
_____
_____
_____
_____

What good, beautiful, or pleasantly surprising thing happened today?
_____
_____
_____
_____
_____

How can you/did you bring joy to someone else today?
_____
_____
_____
_____
_____

Write out a prayer of gratitude or set positive intentions.
_____
_____
_____
_____
_____

Date   /   /   Su Mo Tu We Th Fr Sa

Today, I am grateful for...

_____
_____
_____
_____
_____

What good, beautiful, or pleasantly surprising thing happened today?

_____
_____
_____
_____
_____

How can you/did you bring joy to someone else today?

_____
_____
_____
_____
_____

Write out a prayer of gratitude or set positive intentions.

_____
_____
_____
_____
_____

Date   /   /   Su Mo Tu We Th Fr Sa

Today, I am grateful for...
_____
_____
_____
_____

What good, beautiful, or pleasantly surprising thing happened today?
_____
_____
_____
_____

How can you/did you bring joy to someone else today?
_____
_____
_____
_____

Write out a prayer of gratitude or set positive intentions.
_____
_____
_____
_____

Date   /   /   Su Mo Tu We Th Fr Sa

Today, I am grateful for...
_____
_____
_____
_____
_____

What good, beautiful, or pleasantly surprising thing happened today?
_____
_____
_____
_____
_____

How can you/did you bring joy to someone else today?
_____
_____
_____
_____
_____

Write out a prayer of gratitude or set positive intentions.
_____
_____
_____
_____
_____

Date   /   /   Su Mo Tu We Th Fr Sa

Today, I am grateful for...
_____
_____
_____
_____
_____

What good, beautiful, or pleasantly surprising thing happened today?
_____
_____
_____
_____
_____

How can you/did you bring joy to someone else today?
_____
_____
_____
_____
_____

Write out a prayer of gratitude or set positive intentions.
_____
_____
_____
_____

Date   /   /   Su Mo Tu We Th Fr Sa

Today, I am grateful for...

What good, beautiful, or pleasantly surprising thing happened today?

How can you/did you bring joy to someone else today?

Write out a prayer of gratitude or set positive intentions.

Date   /   /   Su Mo Tu We Th Fr Sa

Today, I am grateful for...
_____
_____
_____
_____
_____

What good, beautiful, or pleasantly surprising thing happened today?
_____
_____
_____
_____
_____

How can you/did you bring joy to someone else today?
_____
_____
_____
_____
_____

Write out a prayer of gratitude or set positive intentions.
_____
_____
_____
_____

Date   /   /   Su Mo Tu We Th Fr Sa

Today, I am grateful for...
_____
_____
_____
_____
_____

What good, beautiful, or pleasantly surprising thing happened today?
_____
_____
_____
_____
_____

How can you/did you bring joy to someone else today?
_____
_____
_____
_____
_____

Write out a prayer of gratitude or set positive intentions.
_____
_____
_____
_____
_____

Date   /   /   Su Mo Tu We Th Fr Sa

Today, I am grateful for...
_____
_____
_____
_____
_____

What good, beautiful, or pleasantly surprising thing happened today?
_____
_____
_____
_____
_____

How can you/did you bring joy to someone else today?
_____
_____
_____
_____
_____

Write out a prayer of gratitude or set positive intentions.
_____
_____
_____
_____
_____

Date   /   /   Su Mo Tu We Th Fr Sa

Today, I am grateful for...
_____
_____
_____
_____
_____

What good, beautiful, or pleasantly surprising thing happened today?
_____
_____
_____
_____
_____

How can you/did you bring joy to someone else today?
_____
_____
_____
_____
_____

Write out a prayer of gratitude or set positive intentions.
_____
_____
_____
_____

Date   /   /   Su Mo Tu We Th Fr Sa

Today, I am grateful for...

What good, beautiful, or pleasantly surprising thing happened today?

How can you/did you bring joy to someone else today?

Write out a prayer of gratitude or set positive intentions.

Date   /   /   Su Mo Tu We Th Fr Sa

Today, I am grateful for...

What good, beautiful, or pleasantly surprising thing happened today?

How can you/did you bring joy to someone else today?

Write out a prayer of gratitude or set positive intentions.

Date   /   /   Su Mo Tu We Th Fr Sa

Today, I am grateful for...
_____
_____
_____
_____
_____

What good, beautiful, or pleasantly surprising thing happened today?
_____
_____
_____
_____
_____

How can you/did you bring joy to someone else today?
_____
_____
_____
_____
_____

Write out a prayer of gratitude or set positive intentions.
_____
_____
_____
_____
_____

Date   /   /   Su Mo Tu We Th Fr Sa

Today, I am grateful for...

What good, beautiful, or pleasantly surprising thing happened today?

How can you/did you bring joy to someone else today?

Write out a prayer of gratitude or set positive intentions.

Date   /   /   Su Mo Tu We Th Fr Sa

Today, I am grateful for...
_____
_____
_____
_____
_____

What good, beautiful, or pleasantly surprising thing happened today?
_____
_____
_____
_____
_____

How can you/did you bring joy to someone else today?
_____
_____
_____
_____
_____

Write out a prayer of gratitude or set positive intentions.
_____
_____
_____
_____

Date   /   /   Su Mo Tu We Th Fr Sa

Today, I am grateful for...

What good, beautiful, or pleasantly surprising thing happened today?

How can you/did you bring joy to someone else today?

Write out a prayer of gratitude or set positive intentions.

Date   /   /   Su Mo Tu We Th Fr Sa

Today, I am grateful for...
_____
_____
_____
_____
_____

What good, beautiful, or pleasantly surprising thing happened today?
_____
_____
_____
_____
_____

How can you/did you bring joy to someone else today?
_____
_____
_____
_____
_____

Write out a prayer of gratitude or set positive intentions.
_____
_____
_____
_____
_____

Date   /   /   Su Mo Tu We Th Fr Sa

Today, I am grateful for...

_____
_____
_____
_____
_____

What good, beautiful, or pleasantly surprising thing happened today?

_____
_____
_____
_____
_____

How can you/did you bring joy to someone else today?

_____
_____
_____
_____

Write out a prayer of gratitude or set positive intentions.

_____
_____
_____
_____

Date   /   /   Su Mo Tu We Th Fr Sa

Today, I am grateful for...
_____
_____
_____
_____
_____

What good, beautiful, or pleasantly surprising thing happened today?
_____
_____
_____
_____
_____

How can you/did you bring joy to someone else today?
_____
_____
_____
_____
_____

Write out a prayer of gratitude or set positive intentions.
_____
_____
_____
_____
_____

Date   /   /   Su Mo Tu We Th Fr Sa

Today, I am grateful for...

What good, beautiful, or pleasantly surprising thing happened today?

How can you/did you bring joy to someone else today?

Write out a prayer of gratitude or set positive intentions.

Date   /   /   Su Mo Tu We Th Fr Sa

Today, I am grateful for...
_____
_____
_____
_____
_____

What good, beautiful, or pleasantly surprising thing happened today?
_____
_____
_____
_____
_____

How can you/did you bring joy to someone else today?
_____
_____
_____
_____
_____

Write out a prayer of gratitude or set positive intentions.
_____
_____
_____
_____

Date   /   /   Su Mo Tu We Th Fr Sa

Today, I am grateful for...

What good, beautiful, or pleasantly surprising thing happened today?

How can you/did you bring joy to someone else today?

Write out a prayer of gratitude or set positive intentions.

Date   /   /   Su Mo Tu We Th Fr Sa

Today, I am grateful for...
_____
_____
_____
_____
_____

What good, beautiful, or pleasantly surprising thing happened today?
_____
_____
_____
_____
_____

How can you/did you bring joy to someone else today?
_____
_____
_____
_____
_____

Write out a prayer of gratitude or set positive intentions.
_____
_____
_____
_____
_____

Date   /   /   Su Mo Tu We Th Fr Sa

Today, I am grateful for...
_____
_____
_____
_____
_____

What good, beautiful, or pleasantly surprising thing happened today?
_____
_____
_____
_____
_____

How can you/did you bring joy to someone else today?
_____
_____
_____
_____
_____

Write out a prayer of gratitude or set positive intentions.
_____
_____
_____
_____
_____

Date   /   /   Su Mo Tu We Th Fr Sa

Today, I am grateful for...
_____
_____
_____
_____
_____

What good, beautiful, or pleasantly surprising thing happened today?
_____
_____
_____
_____
_____

How can you/did you bring joy to someone else today?
_____
_____
_____
_____
_____

Write out a prayer of gratitude or set positive intentions.
_____
_____
_____
_____
_____

Date   /   /   Su Mo Tu We Th Fr Sa

Today, I am grateful for...

What good, beautiful, or pleasantly surprising thing happened today?

How can you/did you bring joy to someone else today?

Write out a prayer of gratitude or set positive intentions.

Date   /   /   Su Mo Tu We Th Fr Sa

Today, I am grateful for...
_____
_____
_____
_____
_____

What good, beautiful, or pleasantly surprising thing happened today?
_____
_____
_____
_____
_____

How can you/did you bring joy to someone else today?
_____
_____
_____
_____
_____

Write out a prayer of gratitude or set positive intentions.
_____
_____
_____
_____

Date   /   /   Su Mo Tu We Th Fr Sa

Today, I am grateful for...
_____
_____
_____
_____
_____

What good, beautiful, or pleasantly surprising thing happened today?
_____
_____
_____
_____
_____

How can you/did you bring joy to someone else today?
_____
_____
_____
_____
_____

Write out a prayer of gratitude or set positive intentions.
_____
_____
_____
_____
_____

Date   /   /   Su Mo Tu We Th Fr Sa

Today, I am grateful for...

_____
_____
_____
_____
_____

What good, beautiful, or pleasantly surprising thing happened today?

_____
_____
_____
_____
_____

How can you/did you bring joy to someone else today?

_____
_____
_____
_____
_____

Write out a prayer of gratitude or set positive intentions.

_____
_____
_____
_____

Date   /   /   Su Mo Tu We Th Fr Sa

Today, I am grateful for...

What good, beautiful, or pleasantly surprising thing happened today?

How can you/did you bring joy to someone else today?

Write out a prayer of gratitude or set positive intentions.

Date   /   /   Su Mo Tu We Th Fr Sa

Today, I am grateful for...

What good, beautiful, or pleasantly surprising thing happened today?

How can you/did you bring joy to someone else today?

Write out a prayer of gratitude or set positive intentions.

Date   /   /   Su Mo Tu We Th Fr Sa

Today, I am grateful for...
_____
_____
_____
_____
_____

What good, beautiful, or pleasantly surprising thing happened today?
_____
_____
_____
_____
_____

How can you/did you bring joy to someone else today?
_____
_____
_____
_____
_____

Write out a prayer of gratitude or set positive intentions.
_____
_____
_____
_____
_____

Date   /   /   Su Mo Tu We Th Fr Sa

Today, I am grateful for...
_____
_____
_____
_____
_____

What good, beautiful, or pleasantly surprising thing happened today?
_____
_____
_____
_____
_____

How can you/did you bring joy to someone else today?
_____
_____
_____
_____
_____

Write out a prayer of gratitude or set positive intentions.
_____
_____
_____
_____
_____

Date   /   /   Su Mo Tu We Th Fr Sa

Today, I am grateful for...
_____
_____
_____
_____
_____

What good, beautiful, or pleasantly surprising thing happened today?
_____
_____
_____
_____
_____

How can you/did you bring joy to someone else today?
_____
_____
_____
_____
_____

Write out a prayer of gratitude or set positive intentions.
_____
_____
_____
_____

Date   /   /   Su Mo Tu We Th Fr Sa

Today, I am grateful for...

_____
_____
_____
_____
_____

What good, beautiful, or pleasantly surprising thing happened today?

_____
_____
_____
_____
_____

How can you/did you bring joy to someone else today?

_____
_____
_____
_____
_____

Write out a prayer of gratitude or set positive intentions.

_____
_____
_____
_____
_____

Date   /   /   Su Mo Tu We Th Fr Sa

Today, I am grateful for...
_____
_____
_____
_____
_____

What good, beautiful, or pleasantly surprising thing happened today?
_____
_____
_____
_____
_____

How can you/did you bring joy to someone else today?
_____
_____
_____
_____
_____

Write out a prayer of gratitude or set positive intentions.
_____
_____
_____
_____

Date   /   /   Su Mo Tu We Th Fr Sa

Today, I am grateful for...
_____
_____
_____
_____
_____

What good, beautiful, or pleasantly surprising thing happened today?
_____
_____
_____
_____
_____

How can you/did you bring joy to someone else today?
_____
_____
_____
_____
_____

Write out a prayer of gratitude or set positive intentions.
_____
_____
_____
_____

Date   /   /   Su Mo Tu We Th Fr Sa

Today, I am grateful for...

What good, beautiful, or pleasantly surprising thing happened today?

How can you/did you bring joy to someone else today?

Write out a prayer of gratitude or set positive intentions.

Date   /   /   Su Mo Tu We Th Fr Sa

Today, I am grateful for...
_____
_____
_____
_____
_____

What good, beautiful, or pleasantly surprising thing happened today?
_____
_____
_____
_____
_____

How can you/did you bring joy to someone else today?
_____
_____
_____
_____
_____

Write out a prayer of gratitude or set positive intentions.
_____
_____
_____
_____
_____

Date   /   /   Su Mo Tu We Th Fr Sa

Today, I am grateful for...

What good, beautiful, or pleasantly surprising thing happened today?

How can you/did you bring joy to someone else today?

Write out a prayer of gratitude or set positive intentions.

Date   /   /   Su Mo Tu We Th Fr Sa

Today, I am grateful for...
_____
_____
_____
_____

What good, beautiful, or pleasantly surprising thing happened today?
_____
_____
_____
_____

How can you/did you bring joy to someone else today?
_____
_____
_____
_____

Write out a prayer of gratitude or set positive intentions.
_____
_____
_____
_____

Date   /   /   Su Mo Tu We Th Fr Sa

Today, I am grateful for...
_____
_____
_____
_____
_____

What good, beautiful, or pleasantly surprising thing happened today?
_____
_____
_____
_____
_____

How can you/did you bring joy to someone else today?
_____
_____
_____
_____
_____

Write out a prayer of gratitude or set positive intentions.
_____
_____
_____
_____

Date   /   /   Su Mo Tu We Th Fr Sa

Today, I am grateful for...
_____
_____
_____
_____
_____

What good, beautiful, or pleasantly surprising thing happened today?
_____
_____
_____
_____
_____

How can you/did you bring joy to someone else today?
_____
_____
_____
_____
_____

Write out a prayer of gratitude or set positive intentions.
_____
_____
_____
_____

Date   /   /   Su Mo Tu We Th Fr Sa

Today, I am grateful for...

What good, beautiful, or pleasantly surprising thing happened today?

How can you/did you bring joy to someone else today?

Write out a prayer of gratitude or set positive intentions.

Date   /   /   Su Mo Tu We Th Fr Sa

Today, I am grateful for...
_____
_____
_____
_____
_____

What good, beautiful, or pleasantly surprising thing happened today?
_____
_____
_____
_____
_____

How can you/did you bring joy to someone else today?
_____
_____
_____
_____
_____

Write out a prayer of gratitude or set positive intentions.
_____
_____
_____
_____

Date   /   /   Su Mo Tu We Th Fr Sa

Today, I am grateful for...
_____
_____
_____
_____
_____

What good, beautiful, or pleasantly surprising thing happened today?
_____
_____
_____
_____
_____

How can you/did you bring joy to someone else today?
_____
_____
_____
_____
_____

Write out a prayer of gratitude or set positive intentions.
_____
_____
_____
_____
_____

Date   /   /   Su Mo Tu We Th Fr Sa

Today, I am grateful for...

What good, beautiful, or pleasantly surprising thing happened today?

How can you/did you bring joy to someone else today?

Write out a prayer of gratitude or set positive intentions.

Date   /   /   Su Mo Tu We Th Fr Sa

Today, I am grateful for...
_____
_____
_____
_____
_____

What good, beautiful, or pleasantly surprising thing happened today?
_____
_____
_____
_____
_____

How can you/did you bring joy to someone else today?
_____
_____
_____
_____
_____

Write out a prayer of gratitude or set positive intentions.
_____
_____
_____
_____

Date   /   /   Su Mo Tu We Th Fr Sa

Today, I am grateful for...
_____
_____
_____
_____
_____

What good, beautiful, or pleasantly surprising thing happened today?
_____
_____
_____
_____
_____

How can you/did you bring joy to someone else today?
_____
_____
_____
_____
_____

Write out a prayer of gratitude or set positive intentions.
_____
_____
_____
_____
_____

Date   /   /   Su Mo Tu We Th Fr Sa

Today, I am grateful for...

What good, beautiful, or pleasantly surprising thing happened today?

How can you/did you bring joy to someone else today?

Write out a prayer of gratitude or set positive intentions.

Date   /   /   Su Mo Tu We Th Fr Sa

Today, I am grateful for...

_____
_____
_____
_____
_____

What good, beautiful, or pleasantly surprising thing happened today?

_____
_____
_____
_____
_____

How can you/did you bring joy to someone else today?

_____
_____
_____
_____
_____

Write out a prayer of gratitude or set positive intentions.

_____
_____
_____
_____
_____

Date   /   /   Su Mo Tu We Th Fr Sa

Today, I am grateful for...
_____
_____
_____
_____
_____

What good, beautiful, or pleasantly surprising thing happened today?
_____
_____
_____
_____
_____

How can you/did you bring joy to someone else today?
_____
_____
_____
_____
_____

Write out a prayer of gratitude or set positive intentions.
_____
_____
_____
_____
_____

Date   /   /   Su Mo Tu We Th Fr Sa

Today, I am grateful for...

_____
_____
_____
_____
_____

What good, beautiful, or pleasantly surprising thing happened today?

_____
_____
_____
_____
_____

How can you/did you bring joy to someone else today?

_____
_____
_____
_____
_____

Write out a prayer of gratitude or set positive intentions.

_____
_____
_____
_____
_____

Date   /   /   Su Mo Tu We Th Fr Sa

Today, I am grateful for...

What good, beautiful, or pleasantly surprising thing happened today?

How can you/did you bring joy to someone else today?

Write out a prayer of gratitude or set positive intentions.

Date   /   /   Su Mo Tu We Th Fr Sa

Today, I am grateful for...

_____
_____
_____
_____

What good, beautiful, or pleasantly surprising thing happened today?

_____
_____
_____
_____

How can you/did you bring joy to someone else today?

_____
_____
_____
_____

Write out a prayer of gratitude or set positive intentions.

_____
_____
_____
_____

Date   /   /   Su Mo Tu We Th Fr Sa

Today, I am grateful for...
_____
_____
_____
_____
_____

What good, beautiful, or pleasantly surprising thing happened today?
_____
_____
_____
_____
_____

How can you/did you bring joy to someone else today?
_____
_____
_____
_____
_____

Write out a prayer of gratitude or set positive intentions.
_____
_____
_____
_____
_____

Date   /   /   Su Mo Tu We Th Fr Sa

Today, I am grateful for...

_____
_____
_____
_____
_____

What good, beautiful, or pleasantly surprising thing happened today?

_____
_____
_____
_____
_____

How can you/did you bring joy to someone else today?

_____
_____
_____
_____
_____

Write out a prayer of gratitude or set positive intentions.

_____
_____
_____
_____
_____

Date   /   /   Su Mo Tu We Th Fr Sa

Today, I am grateful for...

What good, beautiful, or pleasantly surprising thing happened today?

How can you/did you bring joy to someone else today?

Write out a prayer of gratitude or set positive intentions.

Date   /   /   Su Mo Tu We Th Fr Sa

Today, I am grateful for...
_____
_____
_____
_____
_____

What good, beautiful, or pleasantly surprising thing happened today?
_____
_____
_____
_____
_____

How can you/did you bring joy to someone else today?
_____
_____
_____
_____
_____

Write out a prayer of gratitude or set positive intentions.
_____
_____
_____
_____

Date   /   /   Su Mo Tu We Th Fr Sa

Today, I am grateful for...
_____
_____
_____
_____
_____

What good, beautiful, or pleasantly surprising thing happened today?
_____
_____
_____
_____
_____

How can you/did you bring joy to someone else today?
_____
_____
_____
_____
_____

Write out a prayer of gratitude or set positive intentions.
_____
_____
_____
_____
_____

Date   /   /   Su Mo Tu We Th Fr Sa

Today, I am grateful for...

What good, beautiful, or pleasantly surprising thing happened today?

How can you/did you bring joy to someone else today?

Write out a prayer of gratitude or set positive intentions.

Date   /   /   Su Mo Tu We Th Fr Sa

Today, I am grateful for...

What good, beautiful, or pleasantly surprising thing happened today?

How can you/did you bring joy to someone else today?

Write out a prayer of gratitude or set positive intentions.

Date   /   /   Su Mo Tu We Th Fr Sa

Today, I am grateful for...
_____
_____
_____
_____
_____

What good, beautiful, or pleasantly surprising thing happened today?
_____
_____
_____
_____
_____

How can you/did you bring joy to someone else today?
_____
_____
_____
_____
_____

Write out a prayer of gratitude or set positive intentions.
_____
_____
_____
_____
_____

Date   /   /   Su Mo Tu We Th Fr Sa

Today, I am grateful for...
_____
_____
_____
_____
_____

What good, beautiful, or pleasantly surprising thing happened today?
_____
_____
_____
_____
_____

How can you/did you bring joy to someone else today?
_____
_____
_____
_____
_____

Write out a prayer of gratitude or set positive intentions.
_____
_____
_____
_____

Date   /   /   Su Mo Tu We Th Fr Sa

Today, I am grateful for...
_____
_____
_____
_____
_____

What good, beautiful, or pleasantly surprising thing happened today?
_____
_____
_____
_____
_____

How can you/did you bring joy to someone else today?
_____
_____
_____
_____
_____

Write out a prayer of gratitude or set positive intentions.
_____
_____
_____
_____
_____

Date   /   /   Su Mo Tu We Th Fr Sa

Today, I am grateful for...

What good, beautiful, or pleasantly surprising thing happened today?

How can you/did you bring joy to someone else today?

Write out a prayer of gratitude or set positive intentions.

Date   /   /   Su Mo Tu We Th Fr Sa

Today, I am grateful for...

What good, beautiful, or pleasantly surprising thing happened today?

How can you/did you bring joy to someone else today?

Write out a prayer of gratitude or set positive intentions.

Date   /   /   Su Mo Tu We Th Fr Sa

Today, I am grateful for...
_____
_____
_____
_____
_____

What good, beautiful, or pleasantly surprising thing happened today?
_____
_____
_____
_____
_____

How can you/did you bring joy to someone else today?
_____
_____
_____
_____
_____

Write out a prayer of gratitude or set positive intentions.
_____
_____
_____
_____
_____

Date   /   /   Su Mo Tu We Th Fr Sa

Today, I am grateful for...

_____
_____
_____
_____
_____

What good, beautiful, or pleasantly surprising thing happened today?

_____
_____
_____
_____
_____

How can you/did you bring joy to someone else today?

_____
_____
_____
_____
_____

Write out a prayer of gratitude or set positive intentions.

_____
_____
_____
_____

Date   /   /   Su Mo Tu We Th Fr Sa

Today, I am grateful for...
___
___
___
___
___

What good, beautiful, or pleasantly surprising thing happened today?
___
___
___
___
___

How can you/did you bring joy to someone else today?
___
___
___
___
___

Write out a prayer of gratitude or set positive intentions.
___
___
___
___

Date   /   /   Su Mo Tu We Th Fr Sa

Today, I am grateful for...

What good, beautiful, or pleasantly surprising thing happened today?

How can you/did you bring joy to someone else today?

Write out a prayer of gratitude or set positive intentions.

Date   /   /   Su Mo Tu We Th Fr Sa

Today, I am grateful for...
_____
_____
_____
_____

What good, beautiful, or pleasantly surprising thing happened today?
_____
_____
_____
_____

How can you/did you bring joy to someone else today?
_____
_____
_____
_____

Write out a prayer of gratitude or set positive intentions.
_____
_____
_____
_____

I will be *Forever* GRATEFUL.

Made in the USA
Columbia, SC
13 September 2023